MEMOIR OF
TILLIE PIERCE

AN
EYEWITNESS TO THE
BATTLE OF GETTYSBURG

by Pamela Dell

Content Adviser:
Brett Barker, PhD
Associate Professor of History
University of Wisconsin-Marathon County

CAPSTONE PRESS
a capstone imprint

Fact Finders are published by Capstone Press,
1710 Roe Crest Drive, North Mankato, Minnesota 56003
www.mycapstone.com

Library of Congress Cataloging-in-Publication Data
Names: Dell, Pamela, author. | Abridgement of (work): Alleman, Tillie Pierce. At Gettysburg. | Adaptation of (work): Alleman, Tillie Pierce. At Gettysburg.
Title: Memoir of Tillie Pierce : an eyewitness to the Battle of Gettysburg / by Pamela Dell.
Description: North Mankato, Minnesota : Capstone Press, 2017. | Series: Fact finders. First-person histories | Includes bibliographical references and index.
Identifiers: LCCN 2016038564| ISBN 9781515733553 (library binding) | ISBN 9781515733577 (paperback) | ISBN 9781515733591 (ebook pdf)
Subjects: LCSH: Alleman, Tillie Pierce. At Gettsyburg. | Gettysburg, Battle of, Gettysburg, Pa., 1863—Juvenile literature. | Gettysburg (Pa.)—History—Civil War, 1861-1865—Juvenile literature. | Alleman, Tillie Pierce—Juvenile literature.
Classification: LCC E475.53 .D45 2017 | DDC 973.7/349—dc23
LC record available at https://lccn.loc.gov/2016038564

Editorial Credits
Catherine Neitge, editor; Bobbie Nuytten and Catherine Neitge, designers; Svetlana Zhurkin, media researcher; Kathy McColley, production specialist

Photo Credits
Alamy: ClassicStock, 11, Niday Picture Library, 21; CriaImages: Jay Robert Nash Collection, 29 (top); Dreamstime: James Fowler, 4–5, 8–9; Library of Congress, cover (inset on the left), 7, 10, 13, 14, 17, 22–23, 27, 28, 29 (bottom); Newscom: Everett Collection, 15; North Wind Picture Archives, 19; Shutterstock: Atomazul, 25, Everett Historical, 24; Special Collections & College Archives, Musselman Library, Gettysburg College, cover (right), 1, 5; XNR Productions, 9; design elements by Shutterstock

Editor's Note
This book contains only portions of Tillie Pierce's memoir. *At Gettysburg, or, What a Girl Saw and Heard of the Battle. A True Narrative* was published in 1889. It is available online at http://digital.library.upenn.edu/women/alleman/gettysburg/gettysburg.html

Printed and bound in the United States of America.
10029S17

TABLE OF CONTENTS

A Brave Gettysburg Girl

Matilda "Tillie" Jane Pierce turned 15 years old in 1863. She had lived in Gettysburg, Pennsylvania, since her birth. But in that summer of 1863, Tillie witnessed one of the most intense battles of the Civil War—the Battle of Gettysburg. The battle broke out near her home on July 1 and lasted three days. During that time Tillie provided food and water to northern soldiers. She helped nurse the wounded and dying. It was an event she would remember for the rest of her life.

The Civil War, which broke out in 1861, was fought to decide what kind of nation the United States would be. Eleven southern states had **seceded** and formed their own government, the Confederate States of America. The **economy** of the South was based on farming, and many farmers felt they needed enslaved workers to successfully grow crops. The Confederacy went to war to keep their states' rights, the most important of which was their right to own slaves. Many southerners feared that President Abraham Lincoln would take away that right.

The northern states, called the Union, went to war to keep the United States together as one nation. And by 1863 the Union was also fighting to end slavery.

Most Civil War battles took place in the South. But Confederate general Robert E. Lee finally decided to invade the North. If successful, he believed, the Confederacy might destroy the Union army and even capture Washington, D.C. That, he thought, would lead to victory and independence for the Confederacy. But it didn't happen. After a huge battle in Gettysburg, the Union troops won and Lee and his soldiers had to retreat back to Virginia.

Many lives were lost, but the battle was a turning point in the war. Union troops could no longer be stopped. In the two years after Gettysburg, Union armies won more battles. They slowly occupied the South and destroyed Confederate armies. The North triumphed in 1865. The United States remained unified and slavery ended.

As an adult, Tillie Pierce wrote of her dramatic experience during the Battle of Gettysburg. These are her words.

Tillie Pierce

secede—to formally withdraw from a nation or group, often to form another nation

economy—the way a country produces, distributes, and uses its money, goods, natural resources, and services

Tuesday, June 30—

A little before noon ... a great number of Union cavalry began to arrive in the town. They passed ... in the direction of the Theological Seminary.

It was to me a novel and grand sight. I had never seen so many soldiers at one time. They were Union soldiers and that was enough for me, for I then knew we had protection, and I felt they were our dearest friends. I afterwards learned that these men were Buford's **cavalry,** numbering about six thousand men.

> General John Buford is known as the commander who decided the ground on which the Gettysburg battle would be fought. He was the first commander on the scene, leading the 1st Cavalry division of the Union army, which included more than 2,000 men. Many other Union troops also marched in on the day before the battle. Major General George Meade was commander of the entire Union army.

This collection of memoir entries was written by Tillie Pierce 25 years after the dramatic days she spent witnessing the Battle of Gettysburg. Most of the entries are written as vivid recollections of her experiences during the three-day battle. Because Tillie's memoir appears in its original form, you may find a few misspellings and uncommon expressions. To make the meanings of these words more clear, explanations within a set of brackets follow. Also, in some places, words have been removed from the memoir entries. In these cases, you will notice three dots in a row, called ellipses. They show that words or sentences are missing from the text.

A crowd of "us girls" were standing on the corner of Washington and High Streets as these soldiers passed by. Desiring to encourage them, who, as we were told, would before long be in battle, my sister started to sing the old war song "Our Union Forever." As some of us did not know the whole of the piece we kept repeating the chorus.

Thus we sought to cheer our brave men; and we felt amply repaid when we saw that our efforts were appreciated. Their countenances [faces] brightened and we received their thanks and cheers.

The movements of this day in addition to what we beheld a few days previous, told plainly that some great military event was coming pretty close to us. The town was all astir and every one was anxious.

The Lutheran Theological Seminary, where students trained to become ministers, sat on high ground. General Buford used the small domed room at the top of the building as a lookout. From there he had a clear view in every direction.

calvary—soldiers who travel and fight on horseback

Wednesday, July 1—

We awoke early. It was impossible to become drowsy with the events of the previous day uppermost in our minds. We were prompt enough at breakfast that morning.

As more soldiers were expected, and in order to show how welcome they would be, my sister and I had, on the previous evening, prepared a tableful of bo[u]quets which we intended to hand or throw to them as they passed our house.

We had no sooner finished our breakfast when it was announced that troops were coming. We hastened up what we called the side street, (Breckenridge) and on reaching Washington Street, again saw some of our army passing.

First came a long line of cavalry, then wagon after wagon passed by for quite awhile. Again we sang patriotic songs as they moved along. Some of these wagons were filled with stretchers and other articles; in others we noticed soldiers reclining [lying down], who were doubtless in some way disabled.

It was between nine and ten o'clock when we first noticed firing in the direction of Seminary Ridge. At first the sound was faint, then it grew louder. Soon the booming of cannon was heard, then great clouds of smoke were seen rising beyond the ridge. The sound became louder and louder, and was now incessant [continuing without pause]. The troops passing us moved faster, the men had now become excited and urged on their horses. The battle was waging. This was my first terrible experience.

Confederate troops took positions along the high ridge named for the theological seminary. Confederate general Robert E. Lee commanded his troops from there after the first day of battle.

I remember hearing some of the soldiers remarking that there was no telling how soon some of them would be brought back in those ambulances, or carried on the stretchers. I hardly knew what it meant, but I learned afterward, even before the day had passed.

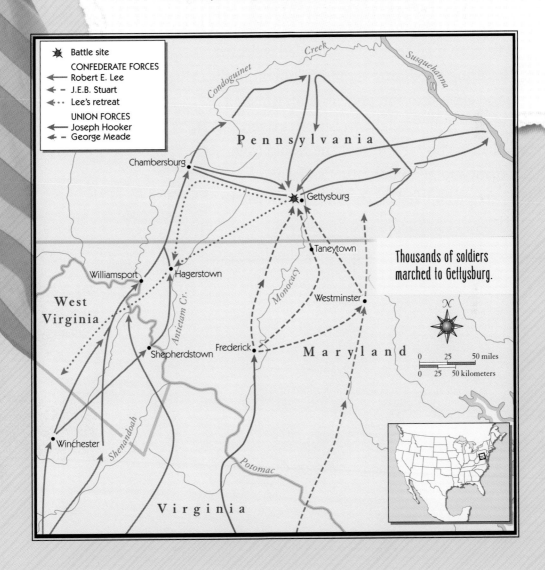

Battle site

CONFEDERATE FORCES
Robert E. Lee
J.E.B. Stuart
Lee's retreat

UNION FORCES
Joseph Hooker
George Meade

Thousands of soldiers marched to Gettysburg.

Pennsylvania

Chambersburg

Gettysburg

Taneytown

Williamsport   Hagerstown

West Virginia

Westminster

Shepherdstown   Frederick

Maryland

0   25   50 miles
0   25   50 kilometers

Winchester

Virginia

Wednesday, July 1—

It was almost noon when the last of the train had passed and I began to think of dinner and the folks at home.

I hurried back, and the first thing that met my gaze as I passed the parlor was the table full of flowers. The soldiers had passed and we had not given them the bo[u]quets. They did not come by our house and in our haste to see them, we had forgotten all about the intended welcome.

Entering the dining-room I found dinner waiting, but I was too excited to eat, and so, soon finished my meal. ...[O]ur neighbor, Mrs. Schriver, called at the house and said she would leave the town and go to her father's (Jacob Weikert), who lived on the Taneytown road at the eastern slope of the Round Top.

little Round Top and Big Round Top are two rocky hills that lie about 3 miles (4.8 kilometers) south of Gettysburg. little Round Top was the site of one of the battle's fiercest fights. On the second day of battle, Union troops took command of the hill and drove off the enemy in a decisive victory.

Little Round Top

Mr. Schriver, her husband, was then serving in the Union army, so that under all the circumstances at this time surrounding her, Mrs. Schriver did not feel safe in the house.

As the battle had commenced and was still progressing at the west of the town, and was not very far off, she thought it safer for herself and two children to go to her parents who lived about three miles to the south. She requested that I be permitted to accompany her, and as it was regarded a safer place for me than to remain in town, my parents readily consented that I should go.

The only preparation I made for the departure, was to carry my best clothes down to the cellar, so that they might be safe when I returned; never thinking of taking any along, nor how long I would stay.

Union soldiers successfully defended Little Round Top to win a key victory in the Battle of Gettysburg.

Wednesday, July 1—

About one o'clock we started on foot; the battle still going on. We proceeded out Baltimore Street and entered the Evergreen Cemetery. This was our easiest and most direct route, as it would bring us to the Taneytown road a little further on.

As we were passing along the Cemetery hill, our men were already planting cannon.

They told us to hurry as fast as possible; that we were in great danger of being shot by the Rebels, whom they expected would **shell** toward us at any moment. We fairly ran to get out of this new danger.

As I looked toward the Seminary Ridge I could see and hear the confusion of the battle. Troops moving hither and thither; the smoke of the conflict arising from the fields; shells bursting in the air, together with the din, rising and falling in mighty undulations [waves]. These things, beheld for the first time, filled my soul with the greatest **apprehensions**.

Rebels were Confederate soldiers, who rebelled against the United States. Union soldiers and other northerners were called Yankees.

shell—to fire metal, gunpowder-filled containers from a large gun

apprehension—the state of being worried and slightly afraid

A Union soldier posed with a Napoleon cannon.

Weapons of War

Union soldiers successfully used several types of cannons at Gettysburg. These big guns were mounted on two wheels, making them easy to move and position.

The popular bronze "Napoleon" was considered a light gun, but it weighed about 1,200 pounds (544 kilograms) and fired 12-pound (5.4-kg) lead balls. Some Confederate troops could only get older model cannons, like the Howitzer, built in the 1840s.

Wednesday, July 1—

It was toward the close of the afternoon of this day that some of the wounded from the field of battle began to arrive where I was staying. They reported hard fighting, many wounded and killed, and were afraid our troops would be defeated and perhaps **routed**.

The first wounded soldier whom I met had his thumb tied up. This I thought was dreadful, and told him so.

"Oh," said he, "this is nothing; you'll see worse than this before long."

"Oh! I hope not," I innocently replied.

Soon two officers carrying their arms in slings made their appearance, and I more fully began to realize that something terrible had taken place.

Now the wounded began to come in greater numbers. Some limping, some with their heads and arms in bandages, some crawling, others carried on stretchers or brought in ambulances. Suffering, cast down and **dejected**, it was a truly pitiable gathering. Before night the barn was filled with the shattered and dying heroes of this day's struggle.

rout—defeat in a manner that causes disorder

dejected—sad and depressed

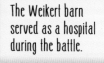

The Weikert barn served as a hospital during the battle.

Thousands died during the three-day battle.

Wednesday, July 1—

That evening Beckie Weikert, [who was] the daughter at home, and I went out to the barn to see what was transpiring [going on] there. Nothing before in my experience had ever paralleled the sight we then and there beheld. There were the groaning and crying, the struggling and dying, crowded side by side, while attendants sought to aid and relieve them as best they could.

We were so overcome by the sad and awful spectacle that we hastened back to the house weeping bitterly. ... The first day had passed, and with the rest of the family, I retired [went to bed], surrounded with strange and appalling events, and many new visions passing rapidly through my mind.

Thursday, July 2—

The day dawned bright and clear; the hot rays of the July sun soon fell upon the landscape.

As quickly as possible I hurried out of the house, and saw more troops hurrying toward town.

The first day's fighting ended in huge loss of life. Of the 50,000 soldiers involved in the battle that day, about 15,500 were killed, wounded, captured, or missing in action.

Horsedrawn covered wagons formed an ammunition train during the Civil War.

About ten o'clock many pieces of **artillery** and large ammunition trains came up, filling the open space to the east of us. **Regiment** after regiment continued to press forward.

I soon engaged in the occupation of the previous day; that of carrying water to the soldiers as they passed.

artillery—large guns, such as cannons, that require several soldiers to load, aim, and fire

regiment—large group of soldiers who fight together as a unit

Thursday, July 2—

...[S]everal field officers came into the house and asked permission to go on the roof in order to make observations. ... I was told to show them the way up. They opened a trap door and looked through their field-glasses at the grand **panorama** spread out below.

By and by they asked me if I would like to look. Having expressed my desire to do so they gave me the glasses. The sight then beheld was wonderful and sublime [awe-inspiring].

The country for miles around seemed to be filled with troops; artillery moving here and there as fast as they could go; long lines of infantry forming into position; officers on horseback galloping hither and thither! It was a grand and awful spectacle, and impressed me as being some great review. ...

It was shortly before noon that I observed soldiers lying on the ground just back of the house, dead. They had fallen just where they had been standing when shot. I was told that they had been picked off by Rebel sharpshooters who were up in Big Round Top.

panorama—wide sweeping view

A Confederate sharpshooter takes deadly aim

Sharpshooters

Expert gunmen called sharpshooters were trained to "pick off" the enemy from hundreds of yards away. Many Union sharpshooters used the Sharps rifle, an extremely fast, accurate weapon that could fire eight to 10 times a minute. This was a great advantage over the more common slow-loading guns.

Rebel sharpshooters used a lower quality "homemade" rifle called the Richmond Sharps. But they often preferred using a Whitworth .45 caliber rifle. It was known as the most accurate long-range rifle of the war.

Thursday, July 2—

Toward the middle of the afternoon heavy cannonading [continuous heavy cannon fire] began on the two Round Tops just back of the house. This was so terrible and severe that it was with great difficulty we could hear ourselves speak. It began very unexpectedly; so much so, that we were all terror-stricken, and hardly knew what to do. ...

The cannonading, which all the time appeared to be getting more and more severe, lasted until the close of day.

It seemed as though the heavens were sending forth peal upon peal of terrible thunder, directly over our heads; while at the same time, the very earth beneath our feet trembled. The cannonading at Gettysburg, has already gone down into history as terrible.

Those who are familiar with this battle now know what **havoc** and destruction were accomplished on this afternoon, on the west side of the Round Tops, at Devil's Den, Sherby's Peach Orchard and the Wheat-field. ...

Between four and five o'clock in the afternoon, I heard some of the soldiers about the house saying: "The Rebels are on this side of Round Top, coming across the fields toward the house, and there will be danger if they get on the Taneytown road." ...

As I went out to the south side of the house I looked in the direction of Round Top, and there saw the Rebels moving rapidly in our direction.

The Pennsylvania Volunteer Reserve Corps, known as the Pennsylvania Reserves, were important to the defense of little Round Top. They were sworn to serve for three years or until the end of the war if it stretched longer. The soldiers fought very hard as they battled to defend their home state.

The Pennsylvania Reserves charged the Rebels on the second day of fighting.

Suddenly I heard the sound of **fife** and drum coming from the other side of the barn.

Then some of our soldiers shouted!:

"There come the Pennsylvania Reserves!" And sure enough there they were, coming on a double-quick between the barn and Round Top, firing as they ran.

The Confederates faced toward them, fired, halted, and then began to retreat. I saw them falling as they were climbing over a stone wall and as they were shot in the open space. The fighting lasted but a short time, when the Confederates were driven back in the direction of Little Round Top. I think they passed between the Round Tops.

On this evening the number of wounded brought to the place was indeed appalling. They were laid in different parts of the house. The orchard and space around the buildings were covered with the shattered and dying, and the barn became more and more crowded. The scene had become terrible beyond description.

havoc—widespread destruction

fife—small flute with a high piercing tone used mainly in military bands

21

Friday, July 3—

The sun was high in the heavens when I awoke the next day. ... Already there was occasional **musketry** and cannonading in the direction of Gettysburg, and we expected greater danger than at any time before.

Some of the soldiers told us that they had planted cannon on two sides of the house, and that if the Rebels attempted to reach the Taneytown road, as they had the day before, there would likely be hard fighting right around the house; and that if we remained, we would be in the midst of flying bullets and shell. Under these circumstances we made all possible haste to depart.

musketry—firing of hand-held guns called muskets by individual soldiers, as opposed to artillery

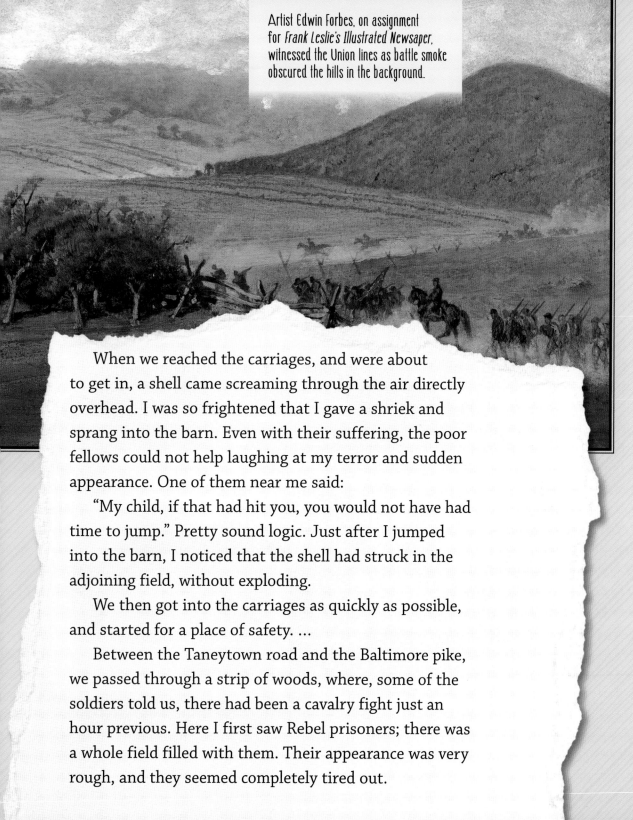

Artist Edwin Forbes, on assignment for *Frank Leslie's Illustrated Newsaper*, witnessed the Union lines as battle smoke obscured the hills in the background.

When we reached the carriages, and were about to get in, a shell came screaming through the air directly overhead. I was so frightened that I gave a shriek and sprang into the barn. Even with their suffering, the poor fellows could not help laughing at my terror and sudden appearance. One of them near me said:

"My child, if that had hit you, you would not have had time to jump." Pretty sound logic. Just after I jumped into the barn, I noticed that the shell had struck in the adjoining field, without exploding.

We then got into the carriages as quickly as possible, and started for a place of safety. ...

Between the Taneytown road and the Baltimore pike, we passed through a strip of woods, where, some of the soldiers told us, there had been a cavalry fight just an hour previous. Here I first saw Rebel prisoners; there was a whole field filled with them. Their appearance was very rough, and they seemed completely tired out.

23

Timothy O'Sullivan's photo of Union soldiers dead in a Gettysburg field was titled *A Harvest of Death*.

Friday, July 3—

Toward the close of the afternoon it was noticed that the roar of the battle was subsiding [letting up], and after all had become quiet we started back for Mr. Weikert's home. As we drove along in the cool of the evening, we noticed that everywhere confusion prevailed. Fences were thrown down near and far; knapsacks, blankets and many other articles, lay scattered here and there. The whole country seemed filled with **desolation**.

desolation—state of complete destruction and emptiness

aghast—filled with horror or shock

prostrate—lying facedown on the ground

Upon reaching the place I fairly shrink back **aghast** at the awful sight presented. The approaches were crowded with wounded, dying and dead. The air was filled with moanings, and groanings. As we passed on toward the house, we were compelled to pick our steps in order that we might not tread on the **prostrate** bodies. ...

Twilight had now fallen; another day had closed; with the soldiers saying, that they believed this day the Rebels were whipped, but at an awful sacrifice.

Deadliest War

The Union won the Battle of Gettysburg, but it cost thousands of lives. Of the nearly 160,000 soldiers involved in the deadliest battle of the Civil War, more than 51,000 were killed, wounded, or captured. The Battle of Gettysburg was the bloodiest combat ever known in North America. The Civil War was the bloodiest four years in U.S. history. It cost at least 620,000 lives, with recent revised estimates putting the figure closer to 750,000.

More than 3,500 Union soldiers are buried in the Gettysburg National Cemetery.

Saturday, July 4—

It was the Fourth of July, and never has the cheering on that anniversary been more hearty and welcome than it was in 1863.

On the summits, in the valleys, everywhere we heard the soldiers hurrahing for the victory that had been won. The troops on our right, at Culp's Hill, caught up the joyous sound as it came rolling on from the Round Tops on our left, and soon the whole line of blue, rejoiced in the results achieved. ... Most befitting was it, that on the fourth of July, an overruling and allwise Providence [God and his will] should again declare this people, free and independent of the tyranny upheld by an enemy. ...

We were all glad that the storm had passed, and that victory was perched upon our banners.

The three days of battle were unbearably hot. The temperatures reached close to 90 degrees Fahrenheit (32 degrees Celsius) on July 3. The next day, July 4, heavy rains drenched the battlefield.

Dark blue was the regulation color for Union soldiers' uniforms. The Confederates chose gray. But with a shortage of regulation uniforms—and cloth itself—many southerners wore their own clothes. Some southern troops wore the uniforms of captured Union soldiers. But first they dyed them in a solution that turned them a tan color people called butternut.

General Robert E. Lee's Confederate army escaped across the Potomac River and back to Virginia.

Turning Point

The Battle of Gettysburg was the turning point of the Civil War. General Robert E. Lee was forced to retreat into Confederate territory. The South was never again able to mount a major offensive against the North. The war raged on for nearly two more years, with the South on the defensive. On April 9, 1865, Lee would surrender to Union general Ulysses S. Grant, ending the bloody war.

But oh! the horror and desolation that remained. The general destruction, the suffering, the dead, the homes that nevermore would be cheered, the heart-broken widows, the innocent and helpless orphans! Only those who have seen these things, can ever realize what they mean.

May the heart of this fair land be forever inclined unto wisdom, so that we may never fall into the folly of another war, and be compelled to pay the fearful penalty that is sure to follow.

About Tillie's Life

In recounting her memories of the Battle of Gettysburg, the adult Tillie assured readers she did not consider herself a heroine. In her book's introduction Tillie wrote that her intention was "simply to show what many a patriotic and loyal girl would have done if surrounded by similar circumstances."

Tillie continued to serve as a nurse in Gettysburg until November 1863 when the last hospital for Union soldiers closed. In 1871 she married a lawyer, Horace Alleman, and moved to Selinsgrove, Pennsylvania, about 85 miles (137 km) from Gettysburg. They had three children. Tillie took part in church and civic activities. Her book *At Gettysburg, or What a Girl Saw and Heard of the Battle*, was published in 1889. Tillie died March 15, 1914.

Timeline

- Dates in Tillie Pierce's life
- Important dates in the Civil War

1848
Tillie Pierce is born.

1861-April 12
The Civil War begins at Fort Sumter, South Carolina, when Confederate soldiers fire on the Union-held fort.

1850 ——————— 1860 —————

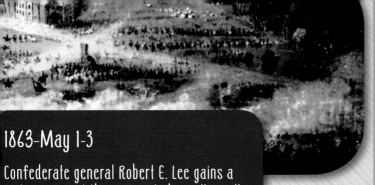

1863-May 1-3

Confederate general Robert E. Lee gains a victory against the Union at Chancellorsville, Virginia, and decides his next move should be to invade the North.

1871-September 28

Tillie marries Horace Alleman.

1914-March 15

Tillie dies.

1863-June 30

General John Buford leads Union troops into Gettysburg and sends word for backup; Lee's forces are also marching in that direction.

1889

Tillie's book, *At Gettysburg, or What a Girl Saw and Heard of the Battle*, is published.

1863-July 1-3

Troops from both sides gather in Gettysburg and begin fighting early on July 1; the battle continues until early evening July 3

1865-April 9

Robert E. Lee surrenders to Ulysses S. Grant, ending the Civil War.

1863-June 3

General Lee begins his second invasion of the North, hoping to win there and even capture Washington, D.C.

1863-November 19

President Abraham Lincoln delivers his famous Gettysburg Address at the newly opened national cemetery.

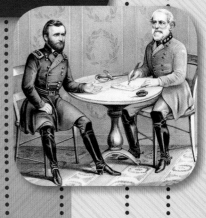

1865

1870

Glossary

aghast (uh-GAST)—filled with horror or shock

apprehension (ap-ri-HEN-shuhn)—the state of being worried and slightly afraid

artillery (ar-TIL-uh-ree)—large guns, such as cannons, that require several soldiers to load, aim, and fire

cavalry (KA-vuhl-ree)—soldiers who travel and fight on horseback

dejected (di-JEK-ted)—sad and depressed

desolation (dess-oh-LAY-shun)—state of complete destruction and emptiness

economy (i-KAH-nuh-mee)—the way a country produces, distributes, and uses its money, goods, natural resources, and services

fife (FYFE)—small flute with a high piercing tone used mainly in military bands

havoc (HAV-ock)—widespread destruction

musketry (MUHSS-kit-tree)—firing of long-barreled guns called muskets

panorama (pan-uh-RAM-a)—wide sweeping view

prostrate (PROS-trate)—lying facedown on the ground

regiment (REJ-uh-muhnt)—large group of soldiers who fight together as a unit

rout (ROWT)—defeat in a manner that causes disorder

secede (si-SEED)—to formally withdraw from a nation or group, often to form another nation

shell (SHEL)—to fire metal, gunpowder-filled containers from a large gun

Read More

Grayson, Robert. *The U.S. Civil War: Why They Fought.*
  North Mankato, Minn.: Compass Point Books, 2016.

O'Connor, Jim. *What was the Battle of Gettysburg?*
  New York: Grosset & Dunlap, 2013.

Tarshis, Lauren. *I Survived the Battle of Gettysburg, 1863.*
  New York: Scholastic, 2013.

Critical Thinking Using the Common Core

1. Tillie was a young and innocent girl when the Civil War reached Gettysburg. On page 9 she writes that she "hardly knew what it meant." Discuss what this statement refers to. Should Tillie have understood more beforehand about what to expect? Why or why not? (Key Ideas and Details)

2. The Confederates had many problems supplying, equipping, and feeding their soldiers. Discuss the reasons why the South was less well-supplied than the North. How did this affect the war's conclusion? (Integration of Knowledge and Ideas)

3. Refer to the map on page 9. Look for symbols that indicate what routes the Union and Confederate troops took to Gettysburg. Discuss whether you think either side had the advantage in where their troops came from. (Craft and Structure)

Internet Sites

Use FactHound to find Internet sites related to this book. All of the sites on FactHound have been researched by our staff.

Here's all you do:

Visit www.facthound.com

Type in this code: 9781515733553

 Super-cool stuff! Check out projects, games and lots more at **www.capstonekids.com**

Index